CW01652128

THE [illegible] Y

DISHES

THE KITCHEN LIBRARY

FISH DISHES

Clare Gordon-Smith

OCTOPUS BOOKS

CONTENTS

This edition published 1988 by
Octopus Books Limited
Michelin House
81 Fulham Road
London SW3 6RB
Reprinted 1988

© Cathay Books 1985

ISBN 0 7064 3239 8
Printed by Mandarin Offset in Hong Kong

INTRODUCTION

With today's emphasis on a healthy diet, what can be better than a natural fresh ingredient that can become a meal in minutes and is also extremely nutritious? Fish is one of the few foods that fits this description.

Take a small white fish, wash it, place a small knob of butter on it, place it under the grill and within minutes you have a ready-portioned meal, without the fuss of trimming or preparation.

Fish can be grilled, steamed, poached in a court bouillon, fried or filled with a tasty stuffing and baked in the oven. They can also take a great variety of sauces to complement their flavour and texture. Choose from the delicious freshly made sauces and savoury butters to bring out the best in your fish dishes.

There are many types of fish available, but don't let this put you off. Instead, welcome it as a wonderful opportunity to make the most of fish and use it to meet some of your dietary needs. Fish is an excellent source of protein, minerals and vitamins. With the wide variety of recipes to choose from, you should be able to please both family and friends at breakfast, lunch and dinner.

NOTES
Standard spoon measurements are used in all recipes.
1 tablespoon = one 15 ml spoon
1 teaspoon = one 5 ml spoon
All spoon measures are level.

Fresh herbs are used unless otherwise stated. If unobtainable substitute a bouquet garni of the equivalent dried herbs, or use dried herbs instead but halve the quantities stated.

Use freshly ground black pepper where pepper is specified.

Ovens should be preheated to the specified temperature.

For all recipes, quantities are given in both metric and imperial measures. Follow either set but not a mixture of both, because they are not interchangeable.

TYPES OF FISH

White fish, such as cod, plaice, hake, turbot, is so called because of its white flesh. It has only a small fat content, so be careful not to dry it out when cooking.
Oily fish such as mackerel, herring, sardines. This has a higher fat content than white fish and is often served with fruity sauces to counteract the fat.
Shellfish falls into two groups:
Jointed shells – crabs, prawns.
Hinged shells – oysters, mussels, clams, cockles.
Freshwater fish such as salmon, trout, carp. These come from lakes and streams.

CHOOSING AND BUYING FISH

Buying fresh fish is easy these days due to the increase in refrigerated equipment, both in transportation and in the fishmongers. Check for the following signs to make sure the fish you are buying is fresh.

- The overall colour should be bright and alive, with the skin shining.
- The eyes should appear bright and bulging with black pupils.
- The gills should be clean and bright red.
- If buying cutlets or steaks the flakes should be firm.
- Fresh fish should have a pleasant odour that you would not find offensive.

PREPARATION OF FISH FOR COOKING

Your fishmonger will be pleased to prepare the fish for you. Always ask for the waste items, such as skin and bones, to use for making fish stock for soups and sauces.

If, however, you do need to skin and fillet smaller fish, such as plaice or Dover sole, it is not difficult. Follow these simple instructions.

To fillet a fish: Place the fish on a board. Run a sharp knife along the centre bone. Scrape along the bones from the head end towards the tail until the fillet is released. Repeat on the other side. Now turn the fish over and remove the other 2 fillets in exactly the same way.

To skin a fillet: Place the fish fillet on a board, tail end towards you, flesh uppermost. Hold the tail firmly. With a sharp filleting knife, keeping the blade as close to the skin as possible, work your way down the fillet.

To skin a whole small fish (so that it can be cooked on the bone): Make a nick in the skin at the tail end, insert a finger and run it up the fish between the skin and the flesh. Ease the skin away from the flesh, pulling towards the head. Repeat this

process on the other side.

If at any time the skin is too slippery to hold, dip your fingers in salt.

To scale a fish, such as red mullet: hold the fish at the tail. Use the back of a knife and scrape towards the head to remove the scales.

To gut a whole fish, such as herring: using a sharp knife, slit open the belly and ease out the guts. Rinse the fish inside and out under running cold water.

COOKING FISH

Fresh fish has a tender delicate flesh. For this reason, fish is cooked to develop its flavour rather than to tenderise it.

Fish therefore needs careful, gentle cooking, over a moderate temperature for a short time. High heat and lengthy cooking times only toughen the flesh and destroy the flavour.

The following methods are the most favourable to fish.

Poaching: Often used for large fish.

Warm the liquid, such as fish stock, milk, water, wine, and add any flavouring, such as bouquet garni, lemon slices, herbs. Place the fish or fillet in the liquid and cook very gently for 10 to 15 minutes for fillets and 8 to 10 minutes per 500 g (1 lb) for whole fish; do not allow to boil.

Steaming: May be used for whole fish and fillets, but make sure they are well seasoned.

Heat some water in a saucepan to simmering point. Place the fish on a buttered plate, cover with another plate, and place on top of the pan. Steam for about 10 minutes.

Grilling: A quick method of cooking fish. Useful for whole fish such as herring and kippers, and fillets such as plaice.

Brush the fish with oil or dot with savoury butter (see page 92) to prevent it from drying. Cook for 5 to 10 minutes, turning the fish over halfway through cooking time.

If grilling whole fish, leave their heads and tails on; this will keep them moist and juicy.

If using fish which is thicker in parts, make diagonal slashes in the thickest parts to allow the heat to penetrate.

Baking: Suitable for whole fish, fillets and steaks.

Place the fish in an ovenproof dish and pour in liquid such as fish stock, wine, milk, water. Add flavourings such as herbs, thinly chopped onion, carrots and celery, and sliced lemon.

Cover with foil and bake in a preheated moderate oven, 180°C (350°F), Gas Mark 4, for 15 to 20 minutes. Remove from the cooking liquid with a fish slice; use the liquid in a sauce.

Braising: This can be done on the hob or in the oven.

Brown some chopped vegetables, eg celery, onion and carrot, in melted butter in a casserole dish. Cut the fish into large chunks or keep in steaks and add to the pan. Pour in about 1.25 litres (2¼ pints) water or stock and 150 ml (¼ pint) wine, cider or vinegar. Add salt and pepper to taste and herbs.

Cook in a preheated moderate oven, 180°C (350°F), Gas Mark 4, for 25 to 30 minutes, or on top of the stove for 20 minutes.

Shallow frying: Suitable for small whole fish, fillets and steaks.

Coat the fish in breadcrumbs, oatmeal, flour or a batter to protect the fish and prevent it from drying out.

Heat enough oil or butter in a large heavy-based frying pan to cover the base and give about 1-2.5 cm (½-1 inch) depth. Add the fish and cook over a moderate heat for 5 to 10 minutes on each side, depending on the thickness of the fish. Drain on kitchen paper.

Deep-frying: Similar to shallow-frying, except the fish is totally immersed in deep oil. Suitable for small whole fish, fillets, steaks and scampi.

Coat the fish as for shallow-frying. Fill a deep pan no more than half full with oil and heat to 180°C (350°F); if a thermometer is not available, drop a cube of day-old bread into the hot oil – if it browns in 60 seconds the oil is hot enough. If the oil is too hot, the coating will brown before the fish is cooked; if it's not hot enough, the coating will be heavy and soggy.

Lower the fish carefully into the hot oil, preferably in a frying basket, and cook for 4 to 8 minutes, depending on the size of the fish. Don't cook too many small pieces at once, e.g. scampi, or the temperature of the oil will be lowered and they will be soggy. Drain on kitchen paper.

TO TEST IF FISH IS COOKED

1. Insert a fork into the fleshiest part of the fish; the flesh will flake away if cooked.
2. The flesh loses its translucence and becomes opaque.
3. A milky curd appears on white fish when cooked.

COURT BOUILLON

A stock in which to braise or poach fish.

2 onions, sliced
3 carrots, sliced
2 celery sticks, sliced
2 lemon slices
25 g (1 oz) bunch of parsley
1 bay leaf
1 tablespoon salt
6 black peppercorns
15 g (½ oz) butter
600 ml (1 pint) dry white wine
1.2 litres (2 pints) water

Place all the ingredients in a pan, bring to the boil, then cover and simmer for 20 minutes. Allow to cool to blood heat before adding the fish.

Once the fish has been cooked, the stock can be strained and used as a basis for sauces for added flavour.

Makes 1.75 litres (3 pints)

FISH FUMET

A concentrated fish-flavoured stock. A good basis for fish soups.

bones and trimmings of 2-3 fish, such as sole, salmon, cod or plaice
2 celery sticks, sliced
2 onions, sliced
1 carrot, sliced
1 bay leaf
1 teaspoon salt
2.5 litres (4½ pints) water
150 ml (¼ pint) dry white wine (optional)

Place all the ingredients in a large pan, bring to the boil, then simmer, uncovered, for 30 to 45 minutes, until reduced to 1.5 litres (2½ pints).

KEDGEREE

This delicious recipe was a traditional breakfast dish among the British in India.

350 g (12 oz) smoked cod fillet
175 g (6 oz) brown rice, cooked
1 egg, hard-boiled and chopped
½ teaspoon paprika
150 g (5 oz) natural yogurt
salt and pepper
25 g (1 oz) butter
lime or lemon wedges to garnish

Place the smoked cod on a plate over a saucepan of simmering water, cover and steam for 7 to 10 minutes, until it flakes when tested. Remove the skin and flake the flesh.

Mix the cod with the brown rice, chopped egg, paprika, yogurt, and salt and pepper to taste. Place in an ovenproof dish and dot with the butter.

Cook in a preheated moderate oven, 180°C (350°F), Gas Mark 4, for 30 minutes. Garnish with lime or lemon wedges to serve.

Serves 4

HAM AND HADDIE

350 g (12 oz) smoked haddock
40 g (1½ oz) unsalted butter
4 small thin slices gammon
parsley sprig to garnish

Divide the haddock into 4 portions and poach in boiling water for 5 minutes. Drain well and remove any skin and bones.

Melt the butter in a large frying pan, add the gammon slices and fry gently for 3 minutes.

Put a piece of haddock on top of each slice of gammon in the pan, cover and cook for 5 minutes.

Transfer to a warmed serving dish, garnish with parsley and serve hot.

Serves 4

VARIATION: For an extra special treat, pour 3 tablespoons double cream over the fish and gammon and place under a preheated hot grill for 2 minutes. Serve immediately.

HERRINGS IN OATMEAL

6 tablespoons medium oatmeal
salt and pepper
4 herrings, cleaned and cut into fillets
15 g (½ oz) butter
1 tablespoon oil
lemon wedges and parsley to garnish

Season the oatmeal with salt and pepper and use to coat the herring fillets. Melt the butter and oil in a frying pan, add 2 fillets at a time and fry for 4 to 5 minutes on each side, until golden.

Garnish with lemon wedges and parsley and serve hot.

Serves 4

CODDLED EGGS

50 g (2 oz) smoked salmon, cut into small pieces
4 eggs
salt and pepper
4 tablespoons double cream
chervil sprigs to garnish

Grease 4 ramekin dishes and divide the smoked salmon between them.

Break an egg into each dish, on top of the smoked salmon pieces. Season with salt and pepper to taste and top each dish with 1 tablespoon cream.

Place the dishes in a roasting pan containing enough water to reach half way up the ramekin dishes.

Cook in a preheated moderate oven, 180°C (350°F), Gas Mark 4, for 10 to 15 minutes or until set. Garnish with chervil and serve immediately.

Serves 4

KIPPERS WITH MARMALADE

1 pair of kippers
15 g (½ oz) unsalted butter
TO SERVE:
orange wedges
1 slice buttered brown bread
1 tablespoon orange marmalade

Remove the head and trim the tail of the kippers with kitchen scissors. Line a grill pan with foil. Place the kippers on the foil, skin side uppermost, and cook under a preheated moderate grill for 1 minute. Turn the kippers over, dot with the butter and grill for a further 5 minutes, until sizzling.

Serve immediately, garnished with orange wedges and accompanied by the brown bread and marmalade.

Serves 1

NOTE: If you don't like the smell of cooking kippers, try this method: place them in a saucepan, cover with boiling water and put on the lid. Simmer for 5 minutes. Drain well.

KIPPER PÂTÉ

This is a good breakfast dish, as it can be made in advance and kept in the refrigerator for several days.

500 g (1 lb) frozen kipper fillets
65 g (2½ oz) unsalted butter
113 g (4 oz) cottage cheese
2 tablespoons lemon juice
pepper
TO GARNISH:
lemon and orange slices
chervil sprigs

Cook the kipper fillets according to packet instructions. Flake the fish slightly, then place in a food processor or electric blender with 25 g (1 oz) of the butter, the cheese, lemon juice, and pepper to taste. Work until smooth.

Divide the mixture between 4 ramekin dishes and smooth the surface. Melt the remaining butter and pour a little over each ramekin. Chill for at least 2 hours before serving.

Garnish with lemon and orange slices and chervil sprigs. Serve with hot wholewheat toast.

Serves 4 to 6

ARBROATH PANCAKES

BATTER:
125 g (4 oz) wholewheat flour
1 egg
300 ml (½ pint) milk
1 tablespoon sunflower oil
FILLING:
350 g (12 oz) tomatoes, chopped
4 spring onions, chopped
1 teaspoon clear honey
pepper
1 arbroath smokie, skinned and flaked
basil leaves to garnish

Place the flour in a bowl, add the egg and gradually beat in the milk until a smooth batter is formed.

Heat the oil in a 20 cm (8 inch) frying pan, pour in about 2 tablespoons of the batter and tilt the pan to coat the base evenly. Cook until the batter has set and the edges are golden brown. Turn the pancake over and cook for a further 20 seconds. Turn onto a warmed plate, cover with greaseproof paper and keep warm. Repeat with the remaining batter to make 6 pancakes.

To make the filling, place the tomatoes, spring onions, honey, and pepper to taste in a saucepan, bring to the boil, then simmer for 5 minutes. Stir in the smokie.

Divide the filling between the pancakes and fold up into triangles. Garnish with basil and serve immediately.

Serves 6

NEW ENGLAND CLAM CHOWDER

50 g (2 oz) butter
2 spring onions, chopped
40 g (1½ oz) plain flour
pinch of cayenne pepper
salt and pepper
600 ml (1 pint) fish stock
1 × 175 g (6 oz) can clams
125 g (4 oz) frozen peeled prawns, thawed
1 × 198 g (7 oz) can sweetcorn, drained
2 potatoes, cubed
142 ml (5 fl oz) soured cream
chopped parsley

Melt the butter in a pan, add the spring onions and fry until softened. Stir in the flour, cayenne, and salt and pepper to taste and cook for 1 minute. Gradually add the stock and bring to the boil. Add the clams, prawns, sweetcorn and potatoes and simmer for 15 minutes, or until the potatoes are soft but still hold their shape.

Stir in the soured cream. Sprinkle with the parsley to serve.

Serves 4

HADDOCK AND MUSHROOM OMELET

25 g (1 oz) butter
125 g (4 oz) mushrooms, sliced
4 eggs, beaten
250 g (8 oz) smoked haddock, steamed and flaked (see Wholewheat Fish Burgers, below)

Melt the butter in a frying pan, add the mushrooms and fry gently for 2 to 3 minutes, until tender.

Add the egg and cook over a low heat for 3 to 4 minutes. When just beginning to set, add the flaked fish and cook for 1 minute. Fold the omelet in half and serve immediately.

Serves 2

HERRING ROES ON TOAST

500 g (1 lb) soft herring roes
2 tablespoons plain flour
salt and pepper
50 g (2 oz) unsalted butter
1 tablespoon anchovy essence
1 teaspoon lemon juice
2 drops Tabasco sauce
½ teaspoon paprika
2 slices wholewheat buttered toast to serve

Place the roes in a colander and pour over boiling water. Dry with kitchen paper. Season the flour with salt and pepper and use to coat the roes.

Melt the butter in a pan until foaming, add the roes and remaining ingredients and fry for about 3 to 5 minutes, until crisp and golden.

Cut the toast into triangles. Put the cooked roe on a warmed serving plate, surround with the toast and serve immediately.

Serves 2 to 4

WHOLEWHEAT FISH BURGERS

250 g (8 oz) smoked haddock
500 g (1 lb) potatoes, boiled and mashed
1 spring onion, chopped
salt and pepper
25 g (1 oz) butter
2 eggs, beaten
50 g (2 oz) wholewheat flour
125 g (4 oz) fresh wholewheat breadcrumbs
2 tablespoons oil

Place the haddock on a plate over a pan of boiling water, cover and steam for 10 to 15 minutes, until the fish flakes easily from the skin. Remove the skin and any bones; flake the fish.

Mix together the potato, fish, spring onion, and salt and pepper to taste. Add the butter and a little of the egg to bind the mixture together. Season the flour with salt and pepper. Shape the mixture into 8 burgers and coat with the seasoned flour. Dip in the beaten egg and coat with the breadcrumbs. Heat the oil in a frying pan, add the fish burgers and fry for 2 to 3 minutes on each side, until crisp and golden. Serve hot.

Makes 8

PLAICE WITH SMOKED SALMON IN LEMON SAUCE

2 plaice, filleted and skinned
50 g (2 oz) smoked salmon, in 2 slices
250 g (8 oz) frozen chopped spinach, thawed
15 g (½ oz) butter
15 g (½ oz) plain flour
150 ml (¼ pint) milk
2 tablespoons lemon juice
salt and pepper
TO GARNISH:
lemon wedges
parsley sprigs

Take 2 plaice fillets and lay a piece of smoked salmon on top of each. Place the remaining fillets on top.

Place the spinach in a buttered ovenproof dish, large enough to hold the plaice side by side. Arrange the fish on top of the spinach.

Melt the butter in a pan, stir in the flour and cook for 1 minute. Gradually stir in the milk and bring to the boil. Stir in the lemon juice, and salt and pepper to taste. Pour over the fish.

Cook in a preheated moderate oven, 180°C (350°F), Gas Mark 4, for 10 to 15 minutes. Garnish with lemon wedges and parsley to serve.

Serves 2

RED MULLET WITH CHICORY

350 g (12 oz) chicory
salt and pepper
25 g (1 oz) unsalted butter
1 small onion, sliced
1 shallot, finely sliced
2 teaspoons lemon juice
salt and pepper
4 small red mullet, cleaned and scaled
TO GARNISH:
dill sprigs
lemon wedges

Blanch the chicory in boiling salted water for 5 minutes. Drain, then break off and slice the leaves.

Melt the butter in a pan, stir in the onion, shallot, chicory, lemon juice, and salt and pepper to taste. Cover and cook for 5 minutes.

Spoon into an ovenproof dish. Place the red mullet on top and sprinkle with salt and pepper. Cover with foil and cook in a preheated moderate oven, 180°C (350°F), Gas Mark 4, for 20 minutes or until cooked. Garnish with dill and lemon to serve.

Serves 4

VARIATION: Replace the chicory with sliced fennel.

TAGLIATELLE WITH SMOKED BUCKLING

250 g (8 oz) dried tagliatelle verdi
1 tablespoon sunflower oil
50 g (2 oz) mushrooms, sliced
250 g (8 oz) Boursin cheese
350 g (12 oz) smoked buckling, skinned, boned and flaked
1 tablespoon chopped parsley to garnish

Cook the tagliatelle according to packet directions.

Meanwhile, heat the oil in a large pan, add the mushrooms and sauté for 3 minutes. Add the cheese and heat gently until melted; be careful not to boil.

Drain the tagliatelle, add to the pan, then stir in the fish.

Garnish with the parsley and serve immediately.

Serves 4

CORNISH EEL

25 g (1 oz) butter
1 onion, chopped
500-750 g (1-1½ lb) conger eel, cut into slices
15 g (½ oz) plain flour
450 ml (¾ pint) dry cider
1 cooking apple, peeled, cored and sliced
2 cloves
salt and pepper
TO GARNISH:
mint or parsley sprigs
lemon slices

Melt the butter in a flameproof casserole, add the onion and fry until softened.

Add the eel pieces and brown lightly. Stir in the flour and cook for 2 minutes, stirring, then gradually pour in the cider, stirring. Add the apple, cloves, and salt and pepper to taste and bring to the boil. Cook in a preheated moderate oven, 180°C (350°F), Gas Mark 4, for 1 hour.

Garnish with mint or parsley and lemon and serve immediately.

Serves 4

CITRUS HALIBUT STEAK

grated rind and juice of 1 orange, lemon and lime
1 halibut steak, cut in half
TO GARNISH:
2 orange, lemon and lime slices

Place 1 tablespoon of each grated rind and all the fruit juices in an ovenproof dish. Add the fish and baste well. Cover and chill for 12 hours, turning the steaks over after 6 hours.

Cover the dish with foil and cook in a preheated moderate oven, 180°C (350°F), Gas Mark 4, for 20 minutes.

Garnish each portion with an orange, lemon and lime slice and serve with mangetouts.

Serves 2

TANDOORI SOLE

½ teaspoon chilli powder
½ teaspoon turmeric
½ teaspoon ground coriander
½ teaspoon ground cumin
1 teaspoon ground ginger
½ teaspoon garam masala
¼ teaspoon salt
pepper
300 g (10 oz) natural yogurt
2 cloves garlic, crushed
2 drops of cochineal
2 lemon sole, skinned and filleted
TO GARNISH:
coriander leaves
lime wedges

Mix all the spices together, adding pepper to taste. Add to the yogurt with the garlic and cochineal and stir until well mixed. Pour into a large bowl, add the fish, turn to coat thoroughly and leave to marinate for 1 hour.

Pour boiling water into a roasting pan to come halfway up the sides. Put a grill rack in the pan and place the marinated fish on the rack. Pour any remaining marinade over the fish.

Cook in a preheated moderate oven, 180°C (350°F), Gas Mark 4, for 15 minutes.

Garnish with coriander and lime wedges and serve immediately.

Serves 2

NOTE: To serve 4 people, just add 2 more fish to the marinade.

STIR-FRIED FISH WITH VEGETABLES

500 g (1 lb) cod fillet, skinned
1 teaspoon salt
1 tablespoon oil
2 rashers back bacon, derinded and shredded
50 g (2 oz) frozen peas, cooked
50 g (2 oz) frozen sweetcorn, cooked
6 tablespoons chicken stock or water
2 teaspoons dry sherry
2 teaspoons soy sauce
1 teaspoon sugar
1 teaspoon cornflour, blended with 1 teaspoon water
spring onion fans to garnish (see right)

Cut the fish fillet into 2.5 cm (1 inch) wide strips, sprinkle with the salt and leave for 15 minutes.

Heat the oil in a frying pan, add the fish and bacon and stir-fry for 3 minutes. Add the remaining ingredients, except the blended cornflour, and bring to the boil. Stir in the blended cornflour and cook for 1 minute.

Garnish with spring onion fans and serve immediately.

Serves 4

TO MAKE SPRING ONION FANS: Trim the tops off the spring onions and remove the root base. Shred carefully, leaving 2.5 cm (1 inch) attached. Immerse in iced water until the spring onions open out and curl.

MUSHROOM-STUFFED PLAICE

4 whole plaice, cleaned
1 tablespoon oil
1 onion, finely chopped
1 clove garlic, crushed
75 g (3 oz) fresh brown breadcrumbs
125 g (4 oz) mushrooms, finely chopped
1 tomato, skinned and chopped
1 teaspoon chopped marjoram
2 teaspoons chopped parsley
dash of Worcestershire sauce
watercress sprigs to garnish

Trim the fish by cutting the fins and tail with a sharp knife. With the white side uppermost, make an incision down the backbone of each fish. Working from each end of the cut in turn, on one half of the fish, cut about two thirds of the way around to form a pocket. Repeat on the other half.

Heat the oil in a pan, add the onion, garlic and breadcrumbs and fry until the breadcrumbs are crisp. Stir in the remaining ingredients and sauté for 2 minutes. Divide the filling between the prepared pockets.

Place the fish in a buttered oven-proof dish and cover with foil. Cook in a preheated moderately hot oven, 200°C (400°F), Gas Mark 6, for 20 to 30 minutes. Garnish with watercress and serve immediately with grilled tomatoes and mushrooms.

Serves 4 to 6

SWORDFISH PROVENÇALE

2 swordfish steaks
1 tablespoon sunflower oil
1 onion, sliced
750 g (1½ lb) tomatoes, thickly sliced
250 g (8 oz) green beans, cut in half
125 g (4 oz) green olives, stoned
2 tablespoons capers
2 teaspoons chopped oregano
MARINADE:
150 ml (¼ pint) dry white wine
4 tablespoons lemon juice
1 small onion, sliced
1 bay leaf
2 thyme sprigs
2 parsley sprigs
2 rosemary sprigs
2 cloves garlic, crushed
salt and pepper
TO GARNISH:
basil sprigs

Cut the swordfish steaks in half, place in a shallow dish and add the marinade ingredients, with salt and pepper to taste. Chill for several hours.

Remove the fish with a slotted spoon; reserve the marinade. Heat the oil in a large pan, add the fish and fry for 5 minutes. Transfer to a casserole dish.

Add the onion, tomatoes, beans, olives, capers, oregano and reserved marinade to the pan and cook, stirring, for 5 minutes. Transfer to the casserole and season with salt and pepper to taste.

Cook in a preheated moderate oven, 180°C (350°F), Gas Mark 4, for 35 to 40 minutes. Discard the bay leaf. Garnish with basil to serve.

Serves 4

HALIBUT WITH RHUBARB

250 g (8 oz) rhubarb, cut into 1 cm (½ inch) pieces
1 tablespoon soft brown sugar
1 tablespoon chopped mint
5 tablespoons dry white wine
2 halibut steaks
salt and pepper
mint sprigs to garnish

Place the rhubarb, sugar and mint in a casserole, then pour over the wine. Place the fish on top, and season with salt and pepper to taste.

Cover and cook in a preheated moderately hot oven, 200°C (400°F), Gas Mark 6, for 15 to 20 minutes, until tender.

Garnish with mint and serve immediately, with creamed potatoes.

Serves 2

SPINACH PANCAKES WITH CRAB

PANCAKE BATTER:
125 g (4 oz) wholewheat flour
½ teaspoon salt
1 egg, beaten
300 ml (½ pint) milk
125 g (4 oz) frozen chopped spinach, thawed
oil for shallow-frying

FILLING:
25 g (1 oz) butter
2 shallots, chopped
1 clove garlic, chopped
125 g (4 oz) mushrooms, sliced
25 g (1 oz) plain flour
300 ml (½ pint) milk
350 g (12 oz) crabmeat
4 tablespoons crème fraîche
4 tablespoons sherry
1 tablespoon grated Parmesan cheese
1 tablespoon chopped chervil
salt and pepper

TOPPING:
25 g (1 oz) butter, melted
1 tablespoon grated Parmesan cheese

TO GARNISH (optional):
whole prawns and dill

To make the batter, place the flour and salt in a bowl, add the egg and half the milk and beat until smooth. Beat in the remaining milk, then stir in the spinach.

Heat a little oil in a 15-18 cm (6-7 inch) frying pan. Pour in about 1½ tablespoons of the batter and cook until the mixture has set and the edges are golden brown. Turn the pancake over and cook the other side. Repeat with the remaining batter, stacking the cooked pancakes on a plate, interleaved with greaseproof paper.

To make the filling, melt the butter in a pan, stir in the shallots, garlic and mushrooms and sauté until soft. Stir in the flour and cook for 1 minute.

Remove from the heat and stir in the remaining ingredients, seasoning with salt and pepper to taste.

Divide the filling between the pancakes, placing it down the middle, and roll up. Place in a shallow ovenproof dish, brush with the melted butter and sprinkle with the cheese.

Cook in a preheated moderately hot oven, 200°C (400°F), Gas Mark 6, for 10 to 15 minutes, until crisp.

Garnish with whole prawns and dill leaves, if using, and serve at once.

Serves 4

PICKLED HERRINGS

6 herrings, cleaned, backbone removed, then cut in half lengthways
2 small onions, sliced and separated into rings
2 dill cucumbers, sliced
MARINADE:
300 ml (½ pint) cider vinegar
300 ml (½ pint) dry cider
1 teaspoon soft brown sugar
2 bay leaves
4 cloves
6 black peppercorns
6 allspice
2 blades of mace
½ teaspoon sea-salt
½ teaspoon cayenne pepper
TO GARNISH:
dill leaves

Place the marinade ingredients in a saucepan, bring to the boil then simmer for 10 minutes.

Lay the herring fillets, flesh side uppermost, on a board. Divide the onion rings and cucumber slices between each fillet, laying along the fish. Roll up from head to tail and secure with a wooden cocktail stick.

Arrange the herring rolls in an ovenproof dish and pour over the marinade. Sprinkle with any remaining onion rings.

Cover with a lid or foil and cook in a preheated moderate oven, 180°C (350°F), Gas Mark 4, for 30 minutes.

Leave in the marinade until cool, then place in the refrigerator. Chill for 1 to 2 days before serving.

Garnish with dill leaves and serve with crusty bread and a green salad.

Serves 6

PRAWNS IN GINGER SAUCE

8 spring onions, chopped
5 cm (2 inch) piece fresh root ginger, chopped
2 tablespoons dry sherry
2 tablespoons soy sauce
150 ml (¼ pint) chicken stock
salt and pepper
12 Mediterranean prawns, peeled

Place all the ingredients, except the prawns, in a saucepan, seasoning with salt and pepper to taste. Bring to the boil, then simmer for 2 minutes. Stir in the prawns, cover and cook for 3 minutes. Serve immediately, with rice or noodles.

Serves 4

SMOKED MACKEREL GOUGÈRE

25 g (1 oz) butter
1 onion, chopped
25 g (1 oz) plain flour
150 ml (¼ pint) milk
3 tablespoons dry cider
2 tablespoons natural yogurt
350 g (12 oz) smoked mackerel, flaked
3 tablespoons chopped watercress
1 small dessert apple, peeled and chopped
salt and pepper

CHOUX PASTRY:
300 ml (½ pint) water
50 g (2 oz) butter
175 g (6 oz) plain flour
4 eggs, beaten
75 g (3 oz) Cheddar cheese, grated
1 teaspoon dry mustard

TOPPING:
1 tablespoon fresh brown breadcrumbs
25 g (1 oz) flaked almonds, chopped

TO GARNISH:
apple slices tossed in lemon juice
mint leaves

Melt the butter in a pan, add the onion and fry until softened. Stir in the flour and milk, bring to the boil, stirring, then simmer for 3 minutes.

Remove from the heat and stir in the remaining ingredients, with salt and pepper to taste. Leave to cool.

To make the choux pastry, place the water and butter in a saucepan and heat gently until melted, then bring to the boil. Remove from the heat, add the flour and beat until smooth.

Return to the heat and beat for 40 seconds, until the mixture leaves the side of the pan and forms a ball.

Remove from the heat and allow to cool slightly, then beat in the eggs a little at a time, beating well after each addition to form a thick glossy dough. Stir in the cheese, mustard, and salt and pepper to taste.

Spoon the choux pastry around the edge of a shallow 1.75 litre (3 pint) ovenproof dish. Place the prepared filling in the centre and sprinkle with the breadcrumbs and almonds.

Cook in a preheated moderately hot oven, 200°C (400°F), Gas Mark 6, for 40 to 45 minutes, until risen and golden. Garnish with apple and mint and serve immediately.

Serves 4 to 6

NOTE: The filling can be made in advance if kept covered and chilled.

SUPPER HERRINGS

4 herrings, filleted
1 tablespoon made English mustard
salt and pepper
1 large onion, sliced
1 large cooking apple, peeled, cored and sliced
½ teaspoon chopped sage
750 g (1½ lb) potatoes, thinly sliced
150 ml (¼ pint) boiling water
sage leaves to garnish

Spread the cut side of the herrings with the mustard, and sprinkle with salt and pepper. Roll them up.

Place a layer of onion in a buttered gratin dish. Cover with a layer of apple and place the herrings on top. Sprinkle with the sage. Cover with the remaining onion and apple and top with a layer of potato.

Pour in the boiling water, cover with foil and cook in a preheated moderately hot oven, 200°C (400°F), Gas Mark 6, for 45 to 50 minutes.

Garnish with sage and serve immediately.

Serves 4

BAKED MACKEREL IN CIDER

1 kg (2 lb) cooking apples, peeled, cored and thinly sliced
5 tablespoons dry cider
150 g (5 oz) natural yogurt
5 tablespoons Dijon mustard
salt and pepper
4 mackerel, filleted
TO GARNISH:
lemon slices
parsley sprig

Spread the apples in a large buttered gratin dish.

Heat the cider gently and pour over the apples. Cover with foil and cook in a preheated moderately hot oven, 200°C (400°F), Gas Mark 6, for 15 minutes. Lower the temperature to 180°C (350°F), Gas Mark 4.

Meanwhile, mix the yogurt with the mustard, and salt and pepper to taste.

Arrange the mackerel in the dish and pour over the yogurt mixture. Return to the oven and cook for 30 minutes.

Garnish with lemon slices and parsley to serve.

Serves 4

QUICK-FRY SALMON

1 tablespoon sunflower oil
1 onion, chopped
500 g (1 lb) potatoes, par-boiled and diced
1 × 439 g (15½ oz) can salmon, drained and flaked
2 tablespoons chopped parsley
125 g (4 oz) frozen peas
pepper
parsley sprigs to garnish

Heat the oil in a pan, add the onion and sauté until soft and transparent.

Add the potatoes and fry for 5 minutes, stirring.

Stir in the salmon, parsley, peas, and pepper to taste. Fry gently for 5 minutes, until heated through. Garnish with parsley and serve immediately.

Serves 4

WHOLEWHEAT FISH CRUMBLE

750 g (1½ lb) halibut
300 ml (½ pint) milk
bouquet garni
salt and pepper
1 celery heart, cut into 1 cm (½ inch) pieces
1 small fennel bulb, diced
2 leeks, sliced
1 carrot, sliced
1 teaspoon grated lemon rind
1 tablespoon lemon juice
150 ml (¼ pint) water
40 g (1½ oz) unsalted butter
40 g (1½ oz) plain flour
3 tablespoons crème fraîche
2 tablespoons chopped parsley
1 teaspoon chopped fennel leaves

TOPPING:
50 g (2 oz) unsalted butter
125 g (4 oz) wholewheat flour
75 g (3 oz) matured Cheddar cheese, grated
½ teaspoon cayenne pepper

Put the fish in a saucepan with the milk, bouquet garni, and salt and pepper to taste, cover and simmer for 10 to 15 minutes, until the fish flakes away from the skin. Remove with a slotted spoon, reserving the cooking liquid. Remove any skin and bones and flake the fish into large pieces.

Place the vegetables in a saucepan with the lemon rind, juice and water. Bring to the boil, then cover and simmer for 5 minutes, until just tender. Drain, reserving the cooking liquid, and set aside.

Melt the butter in a pan, stir in the flour and cook for 1 minute. Gradually stir in the reserved cooking liquids, bring to the boil and boil for 1 minute. Remove from the heat and stir in the crème fraîche, parsley, fennel leaves, fish and vegetables. Pour into a 1.2 litre (2 pint) pie dish.

Rub the butter into the flour until the mixture resembles breadcrumbs. Stir in the cheese and cayenne and sprinkle over the fish mixture.

Cook in a preheated moderately hot oven, 200°C (400°F), Gas Mark 6, for 20 minutes. Serve hot.

Serves 4 to 6

FISH FACES

150 ml (¼ pint) milk
150 ml (¼ pint) water
250 g (8 oz) haddock fillets
salt and pepper
500 g (1 lb) potatoes, boiled and mashed
1 × 213 g (7½ oz) can pink salmon, drained and flaked
125 g (4 oz) tomatoes, skinned and chopped
4 tablespoons chopped parsley
2 tablespoons natural yogurt
75 g (3 oz) fresh wholewheat breadcrumbs
2 tablespoons grated cheese
25 g (1 oz) plain flour
1 egg, beaten
2 tablespoons oil
TO GARNISH:
olive slices
tomato strips
lemon slices

Bring the milk and water to the boil in a large pan, add the haddock and a little salt and pepper and simmer for 10 minutes, or until tender.

Remove any skin and bones from the haddock and flake the fish. Place in a bowl with the potato, salmon, tomato, half the parsley, yogurt, and salt and pepper to taste and mix well. Divide the mixture into 8 and shape each piece into an oval.

Mix together the breadcrumbs, cheese and remaining parsley. Dip the fish cakes into the flour, then the beaten egg, and finally into the breadcrumb mixture to coat completely.

Heat the oil in a frying pan, add the fish cakes and fry for 3 minutes on each side, until golden. Transfer to a warmed serving plate and garnish each fish cake with an olive slice for an eye, a tomato strip for a mouth and lemon slices, quartered, for its tail.

Makes 8

SARDINE PIZZA

1 × 150 g (6 oz) packet pizza base mix
1 × 120 g (4¼ oz) can sardines in oil, drained and mashed
1 × 397 g (14 oz) can tomatoes, drained and chopped
½ teaspoon chopped oregano
salt and pepper
1 green pepper, cored, seeded and sliced
50 g (2 oz) mushrooms, sliced
125 g (4 oz) Mozzarella cheese, sliced
1 × 50 g (1¾ oz) can anchovy fillets, drained
6 black olives

Make up the pizza mix according to packet directions. Roll into an 18 cm (7 inch) circle and place on a baking sheet.

Place the sardines, tomatoes, oregano, and salt and pepper to taste in a bowl and mix well to combine. Spoon onto the pizza base and arrange the green pepper and mushrooms attractively on top. Cover with the cheese slices.

Arrange the anchovies in a criss cross pattern on top and finish with the olives.

Cook in a preheated moderately hot oven, 200°C (400°F), Gas Mark 6, for 20 to 25 minutes.

Serve immediately, with a green salad.

Serves 4 to 6

VARIATION: Replace the sardines with 1 × 99 g (3½ oz) can tuna steak.

STUFFED PEPPERS

500 g (1 lb) cod fillets
300 ml (1/2 pint) boiling water
bouquet garni
1/2 onion
salt and pepper
1 tablespoon sunflower oil
1 onion, chopped
2 celery sticks, chopped
125 g (4 oz) brown rice
1 × 227 g (8 oz) can tomatoes
1 bay leaf
1 teaspoon chopped marjoram
150 ml (1/4 pint) cold water
125 g (4 oz) peeled prawns
4 tablespoons frozen sweetcorn
4 green peppers
TO GARNISH:
marjoram sprigs
whole prawns in shell

Place the fish in a pan with the boiling water, bouquet garni, half-onion, and salt and pepper to taste. Cover and simmer for 10 to 15 minutes.

Remove with a slotted spoon, remove any skin and bones and flake the fish into chunks. Set aside.

Heat the oil in a frying pan, add the chopped onion and celery and fry for 2 minutes. Add the rice and fry for a further 3 minutes.

Stir in the tomatoes, with their juice, bay leaf, marjoram, and salt and pepper to taste. Pour in the cold water, bring to the boil, cover and simmer for 40 minutes, until rice is tender and liquid absorbed. Remove from the heat and stir in the flaked fish, prawns and sweetcorn.

Remove the top from each pepper and reserve. Remove the core and seeds, and trim the base to level. Blanch in a pan of boiling water for 2 minutes, drain and plunge into cold water. Drain well.

Divide the rice and fish mixture between the 4 peppers. Arrange in an ovenproof dish and replace the tops. Cook in a preheated moderate oven, 180°C (350°F), Gas Mark 4, for 15 minutes. Garnish with marjoram sprigs and prawns to serve.

Serves 4

FISH IN WHOLEWHEAT BREADCRUMBS

4 haddock fillets
2 tablespoons plain flour
125 g (4 oz) wholewheat breadcrumbs
2 tablespoons chopped parsley
salt and pepper
1 egg, beaten
oil for shallow-frying
TO GARNISH:
parsley sprigs
lemon wedges

Dip the fillets into the flour.

Mix together the breadcrumbs, parsley, and salt and pepper to taste on a plate.

Dip the fillets into the beaten egg, then into the breadcrumb mixture. Shallow-fry in hot oil until crisp and golden.

Garnish with parsley and lemon and serve with Tartare Sauce (see page 89).

Serves 4

CRISPY TOP COD

300 ml (½ pint) boiling water
bouquet garni
1 onion, roughly chopped
4 chunky cod fillets
75 g (3 oz) Cheddar cheese, grated
450 ml (¾ pint) White Sauce (see page 86)
2 × 25 g (1 oz) packets ready salted crisps
TO GARNISH:
parsley sprigs
lemon twists

Place the water, bouquet garni and onion in a large pan, add the cod and cook for 10 to 15 minutes, until tender. Remove with a slotted spoon and place in a shallow dish.

Stir the cheese into the hot sauce until melted. Pour over the fish. Roughly crush the crisps and sprinkle over.

Cook under a preheated hot grill for 2 to 3 minutes, until golden. Garnish with parsley and lemon and serve immediately.

Serves 4 to 6

MARINER'S PIE

450 ml (¾ pint) milk
1 bay leaf
2 lemon slices
salt and pepper
500 g (1 lb) whiting fillets
50 g (2 oz) butter
125 g (4 oz) button mushrooms, quartered
40 g (1½ oz) plain flour
3 tablespoons yogurt or soured cream
2 tablespoons chopped parsley
2 hard-boiled eggs, chopped
500 g (1 lb) potatoes, boiled and sliced
50 g (2 oz) Cheddar cheese, grated
TO GARNISH:
parsley sprigs

Put the milk, bay leaf, lemon slices, and salt and pepper to taste in a saucepan and bring to the boil. Add the fish and simmer for 10 to 15 minutes, until tender. Remove with a slotted spoon. Strain and reserve the liquid. Flake the fish, removing any skin or bones.

Melt the butter in a pan, add the mushrooms and cook for 2 minutes. Stir in the flour, cook for 1 minute, then gradually stir in the reserved liquid and bring to the boil.

Remove from the heat and stir in the fish, yogurt or soured cream, parsley and chopped egg. Check the seasoning and pour into a 1.2 litre (2 pint) pie dish. Arrange the potato on top, then sprinkle with the cheese.

Cook under a preheated moderate grill for 5 minutes, or in a preheated moderate oven, 180°C (350°F), Gas Mark 4, for 10 to 15 minutes.

Garnish with the parsley and serve immediately.

Serves 4

CREAMED COCONUT MONKFISH

125 g (4 oz) desiccated coconut
300 ml (½ pint) boiling water
750 g (1½ lb) monkfish
1 tablespoon oil
6 spring onions, chopped
3 green chillies, seeded and chopped
1 red pepper, cored, seeded and chopped
1 clove garlic, crushed
5 cm (2 inch) piece fresh root ginger, chopped
½ teaspoon ground cumin
½ teaspoon ground coriander
1 teaspoon grated lemon rind
1 tablespoon lime juice
1 tablespoon sherry
salt and pepper
TO GARNISH:
lime wedges
coriander leaves

Place the coconut in a bowl, pour over the boiling water and leave to infuse for 30 minutes. Strain and reserve the liquid, discarding the coconut.

Meanwhile, cut the fish into 5 cm (2 inch) cubes. Heat the oil in a large pan and stir in the remaining ingredients, except the fish, seasoning with salt and pepper to taste. Add the fish, pour on the coconut milk and bring to the boil, then simmer for 5 minutes.

Transfer to a warmed serving dish, garnish with lime and coriander, and serve with rice.

Serves 4

FISHERMAN'S PIE

350 ml (12 fl oz) milk
1 bay leaf
1 onion, quartered
350 g (12 oz) smoked haddock or cod
350 g (12 oz) fresh haddock or whiting
25 g (1 oz) unsalted butter
25 g (1 oz) plain flour
125 g (4 oz) peeled prawns
125 g (4 oz) frozen peas
2 tablespoons chopped parsley
salt and pepper
2 × 370 g (13 oz) packets wholewheat puff pastry, thawed
beaten egg to glaze
TO GARNISH:
orange wedges
watercress sprigs

Place the milk, bay leaf and onion in a large saucepan and bring to the boil. Add the fish and cook gently for 10 minutes, until tender. Remove with a slotted spoon. Make up the cooking liquid to 350 ml (12 fl oz) with water and set aside.

Remove the skin and bones from the fish and flake the flesh.

Melt the butter in a large pan, stir in the flour and cook for 1 minute. Gradually stir in the reserved cooking liquid until smooth, then bring to the boil. Remove from the heat and stir in the fish, prawns, peas, parsley, and salt and pepper to taste. Leave to cool.

Roll out half the pastry on a floured surface to an oval about 23 × 30 cm (9 × 12 inches). Place on a dampened baking sheet and pour on the cooled fish mixture. Roll out the remaining pastry to the same size and shape and place on top. Trim, reserving any left-over pastry for decoration. Dampen, seal and flute the edge. Make a small hole in the centre and decorate with pastry trimmings. Brush with beaten egg.

Bake in a preheated moderately hot oven, 200°C (400°F), Gas Mark 6, for 30 to 35 minutes. Lower the temperature to 180°C (350°F), Gas Mark 4, and bake for a further 20 minutes. Garnish with orange and watercress. Serve hot.

Serves 4 to 6

SKATE PARCELS

3 tablespoons sunflower oil
2 carrots, sliced into matchstick pieces
3 celery sticks, sliced lengthways
½ fennel bulb, sliced lengthways
8 spring onions, sliced lengthways
1 courgette, sliced lengthways
1 tablespoon soy sauce
1 tablespoon dry sherry
1 tablespoon tomato ketchup
salt and pepper
4 skate wings
orange twists to garnish

Heat 1 tablespoon of the oil in a frying pan, add the vegetables and stir-fry for 3 minutes.

Add the soy sauce, sherry, tomato ketchup, and salt and pepper to taste and simmer for 2 minutes. Set aside.

Heat the remaining oil in another pan, add the skate wings and fry quickly for 2 minutes on each side.

Place each skate wing on a large piece of foil and cover with the vegetable mixture. Fold the foil over to form a parcel and seal well.

Place on a baking sheet and cook in a preheated moderately hot oven, 200°C (400°F), Gas Mark 6, for 15 to 20 minutes, until tender.

Garnish with orange twists and serve immediately.

Serves 4

CARIBBEAN SCAMPI

350 g (12 oz) uncooked scampi
3 tablespoons plain flour
oil for deep-frying
50 g (2 oz) desiccated coconut
BATTER:
125 g (4 oz) plain flour
pinch of salt
2 teaspoons sunflower oil
7-8 tablespoons beer or tepid water
2 egg whites
TO GARNISH:
coriander sprig
lime wedges

First, make the batter. Sift the flour and salt into a bowl, then beat in the oil and beer or water to form a smooth thick batter.

Just before using, whisk the egg whites until soft peaks form, then gently fold into the batter mixture.

Toss the scampi in the flour, then dip into the batter to coat thickly and evenly.

Deep-fry a few at a time in the hot oil for 5 to 7 minutes, until crisp and golden. Drain on kitchen paper, then toss in the coconut.

Serve immediately, garnished with coriander and lime.

Serves 4

MOULES MARINIÈRE

2.25 litres (4 pints) fresh mussels
2 shallots, chopped
1 onion, chopped
50 g (2 oz) chopped parsley
300 ml (½ pint) dry white wine
50 g (2 oz) unsalted butter
salt and pepper
chopped parsley to garnish (optional)

Scrub and clean the mussels, removing any beards. Place in a large saucepan with the shallots, onion, parsley, wine and butter. Bring to the boil, cover and simmer for about 5 minutes, shaking the pan occasionally, until the shells open; discard any that do not. Remove the mussels with a slotted spoon, pile into a warmed serving bowl and keep hot.

Strain the cooking liquid into another pan. Bring to the boil and boil for 1 minute. Season with salt and pepper to taste, then pour over the mussels.

Garnish with parsley, if desired, and serve immediately, with crusty French bread.

Serves 4

MONKFISH KEBABS

500 g (1 lb) monkfish, cubed
2 green peppers, cored, seeded and cut into 2.5 cm (1 inch) squares
1 × 227 g (8 oz) can pineapple pieces
1 tablespoon olive oil
250 g (8 oz) bean sprouts
1 tablespoon soy sauce
salt and pepper
2 spring onions, chopped
MARINADE:
150 ml (1/4 pint) olive oil
1 small onion, chopped
2 cloves garlic, crushed
1 teaspoon Dijon mustard
2 teaspoons cider vinegar

Place the monkfish in a shallow dish. Mix together the marinade ingredients, pour over the fish and leave for 1 hour.

Blanch the green pepper in boiling water for 1 minute. Drain the pineapple and reserve the juice.

Thread the fish, green pepper and pineapple alternately on 8 kebab skewers. Cook under a preheated moderate grill for 5 to 6 minutes on each side, basting with the marinade.

Meanwhile, heat the oil in a large frying pan, add the bean sprouts and stir-fry for 1 to 2 minutes. Add the reserved pineapple juice, the soy sauce, and salt and pepper to taste and heat for 1 to 2 minutes. Transfer to a warmed serving dish and sprinkle with the spring onions.

Place the kebabs on the bean sprout mixture and serve immediately.
Serves 4

HUSS AND WATERCRESS SOUP

600 ml (1 pint) milk
bouquet garni
2 shallots, chopped
250 g (8 oz) huss, chopped
125 g (4 oz) watercress
142 ml (5 fl oz) single cream
TO GARNISH:
watercress sprigs (optional)
croûtons

Place the milk, bouquet garni and shallots in a saucepan, bring to the boil, then lower the heat. Add the huss and watercress and simmer for 8 to 10 minutes, until the fish flakes when tested with a knife. Place in an electric blender or food processor and work until smooth.

Return to the saucepan, stir in the cream and heat gently; do not allow to boil.

Serve in individual warmed soup bowls, garnished with watercress if using, and croûtons.
Serves 4

GRAVAD LAX

750 g-1 kg (1½-2 lb) salmon tailpiece, scaled and filleted
PICKLE:
1 heaped tablespoon sea salt
1 tablespoon sugar
1 teaspoon black peppercorns, crushed
1 tablespoon brandy
1 tablespoon chopped dill
TO GARNISH:
dill leaves
lime slices

Mix together the pickle ingredients in a small bowl and transfer a quarter of the mixture to a flat dish.

Place one salmon fillet, skin side down, in the pickle mixture. Spread half of the remaining pickle over the cut side of the salmon. Place the other piece of salmon, skin side up, on top.

Cover with the remaining pickle mixture, rubbing it into the skin. Cover with foil, lay a board on top and weight it down.

Chill for at least 12 hours before serving; it can be left for up to 5 days.

Drain well and slice the salmon either on the bias for smaller slices or parallel to the skin to obtain larger slices. Garnish with dill and lime slices and serve with Mustard Sauce (see page 88).

Serves 4 to 6

POTTED SHRIMPS

750 g (1½ lb) shrimps in shells, or 500 g (1 lb) shelled shrimps
250 g (8 oz) unsalted butter, clarified (see below)
¼ teaspoon cayenne pepper
½ teaspoon ground mace
½ teaspoon grated nutmeg
salt
TO GARNISH:
lemon slices
chervil sprigs

Shell the shrimps if necessary. Drain the shrimps well and dry with kitchen paper.

Put two thirds of the clarified butter into a saucepan with the spices, and salt to taste. Add the shrimps and heat gently for a few minutes. Divide between 4 to 6 cocotte or ramekin dishes and pack down tightly. Chill until set.

Heat the remaining clarified butter until just melted, then pour evenly over the shrimp mixture to make an airtight seal. Cover and keep in the refrigerator for at least a day to develop the flavour.

Garnish each dish with a lemon slice and chervil sprig. Serve with hot wholewheat toast.

Serves 4 to 6

TO CLARIFY BUTTER: Melt the butter, leave to settle, then strain through muslin.

TARAMASALATA

175 g (6 oz) smoked cod's roe, chopped
113 g (4 oz) curd cheese
50 g (2 oz) fresh white breadcrumbs
2 tablespoons lemon juice
8-10 tablespoons olive oil
pepper
1 teaspoon lumpfish caviar to garnish

Place the cod's roe, cheese, breadcrumbs and lemon juice in a food processor or electric blender and work until smooth.

Gradually add the olive oil with the machine running, and blend until smooth and creamy. Season with pepper to taste. Chill for 2 hours.

Garnish with lumpfish caviar and serve with toast.

Serves 4

SALMON AND MONKFISH MOUSSELINES

125 g (4 oz) asparagus spears, trimmed and blanched
50 g (2 oz) peeled prawns
MONKFISH FILLING:
300 g (10 oz) monkfish, off the bone and trimmed of membrane
2 tablespoons dry white wine
2 tablespoons crème fraîche
2 tablespoons chopped tarragon
1 tablespoon chopped chervil
salt and pepper
1 egg, beaten
SALMON FILLING:
300 g (10 oz) salmon fillet
2 tablespoons crème fraîche
dash of Tabasco

Grease 4 individual loaf tins 10 × 6 × 4 cm (4 × 2½ × 1½ inches) with butter. Arrange the asparagus and prawns attractively in the tins.

Roughly chop the monkfish and place in a food processor or electric blender with the remaining monkfish filling ingredients, adding salt and pepper to taste and half the beaten egg. Work until smooth and divide between the 4 tins.

Place the salmon filling ingredients and remaining beaten egg in the food processor or electric blender and work until smooth. Divide between the 4 tins, placing on top of the monkfish filling.

Cover each tin with foil and place in a roasting pan. Pour in enough boiling water to come half-way up the tins. Cook in a preheated moderate oven, 180°C (350°F), Gas Mark 4, for 15 to 20 minutes or until firm when touched.

Unmould the mousselines onto individual serving plates and serve warm with Hollandaise Sauce (see page 90).

If preferred, chill for several hours, then turn out 30 minutes before required to come to room temperature.

Serves 4

SCALLOPS WITH DILL AND LIME

juice of 2 limes
350 g (12 oz) queens (see below) or scallops
salt and pepper
2 tablespoons chopped dill
1 tablespoon chopped mint
¼ cucumber, diced
2 teaspoons sunflower oil
TO GARNISH:
lime slices
mint sprigs

Pour the lime juice into a saucepan, add the queens or scallops, and salt and pepper to taste. Bring to the boil, then simmer for 2 to 3 minutes, until white in appearance.

Remove from the heat and allow to cool. Add the dill, mint, cucumber and oil and place in a serving dish. Chill for 2 hours to allow the flavours to develop.

Garnish with lime slices and mint sprigs and serve with hot wholewheat toast.

Serves 4

NOTE: Queens are smaller than scallops and are ideal for starter dishes.

MACKEREL AND SPINACH CANNELLONI

175 g (6 oz) smoked mackerel fillets, flaked
113 g (4 oz) cottage cheese
125 g (4 oz) frozen chopped spinach, thawed
salt and pepper
8 tubes cannelloni
300 ml (½ pint) Tomato Sauce (see page 89)
2 tablespoons grated Parmesan cheese

Mix together the fish, cheese, spinach, and salt and pepper to taste. Divide between the cannelloni and place in an ovenproof dish. Pour over the tomato sauce and sprinkle with the Parmesan cheese.

Cook in a preheated moderate oven, 180°C (350°F), Gas Mark 4, for 15 to 20 minutes. Serve hot with a green salad.

Serves 4

FRIED WHITEBAIT

3 tablespoons plain flour
½ teaspoon salt
¼ teaspoon paprika
500 g (1 lb) whitebait
oil for deep-frying
TO GARNISH:
chopped parsley
lemon wedges

Mix the flour with the salt and paprika and use to coat the whitebait.

Deep-fry the whitebait in batches in hot oil for 2 to 3 minutes, until lightly browned and crisp. Drain on kitchen paper and place on a warmed serving plate.

Sprinkle with parsley and garnish with lemon wedges. Serve immediately, with thin slices of brown bread and butter.

Serves 4

CREAMY HADDOCK AND LEEKS

250 g (8 oz) smoked haddock
65 g (2½ oz) butter
2 leeks, sliced
500 g (1 lb) potatoes, boiled and diced
142 ml (5 fl oz) soured cream
salt and pepper
1 tablespoon chopped parsley to garnish

Place the haddock on a plate over a saucepan of boiling water. Dot with 15 g (½ oz) of the butter, cover and steam for 10 minutes or until the fish flakes easily.

Melt the remaining butter in a large pan, add the leeks and cook for 5 minutes, until soft. Add the potatoes and fish, then stir in the soured cream, and salt and pepper to taste.

Garnish with the chopped parsley and serve hot.

Serves 4

HUSS SALAD

500 g (1 lb) huss fillets, skinned
300 ml (½ pint) dry white wine or water
1 onion, roughly chopped
1 bay leaf
salt and pepper
500 g (1 lb) new potatoes, boiled and halved
½ cucumber, diced
1 × 250 g (8 oz) jar pickled sweet baby beetroot, cubed
2 tablespoons capers
DRESSING:
150 ml (¼ pint) Fromage Frais
juice of ½ lemon
2 tablespoons chopped chives
1 tablespoon chopped chervil

Place the fish, wine or water, onion, bay leaf, and salt and pepper to taste in a pan and simmer for 10 to 15 minutes or until the fish flakes easily. Drain, cool and cube the fish.

Place in a large bowl with the potatoes, cucumber, beetroot and capers.

Mix the dressing ingredients together, with salt and pepper to taste, pour over the salad and mix well.

Serves 4

SCAMPI AND AVOCADO SALAD

1 tablespoon olive oil
salt and pepper
250 g (8 oz) scampi
1 avocado pear, peeled, stoned and thinly sliced
2 oranges, peeled and segmented
2 small heads of chicory, separated into leaves
DRESSING:
2 tablespoons olive oil
3 tablespoons orange juice
2 tablespoons lemon juice
1 tablespoon chopped chervil
1 teaspoon chopped chives

Heat the oil in a frying pan and sprinkle in a little salt and pepper. Add the scampi and sauté for 3 to 5 minutes, until white in appearance. Remove with a slotted spoon; reserve the oil for the dressing.

Arrange the avocado, orange and chicory on individual serving plates, with the scampi.

Put the dressing ingredients in a screw-top jar. Add the reserved oil, and salt and pepper to taste and shake well. Pour over the salads and serve.

Alternatively, chop all the salad ingredients, place in a serving bowl, pour over the dressing and toss well.

Serves 4

NOTE: If you want to serve the salad as a main course, increase the scampi to 500g (1 lb).

KIWI TROUT SALAD

175 g (6 oz) smoked trout
2 dessert apples, cored
1 kiwi fruit, sliced
50 g (2 oz) flaked almonds, toasted
2 tablespoons soured cream
1 teaspoon lemon juice
2 tablespoons chopped mint
pepper
4 mint sprigs to garnish

Remove the skin and bones from the trout. Flake the fish into bite-sized pieces and place in a bowl.

Chop the apples and add to the fish with the kiwi fruit, almonds, soured cream, lemon juice, chopped mint, and pepper to taste.

Mix well, divide between 4 serving plates and garnish with a mint sprig.

Serves 4

NOTE: If you want to serve this as a main course, double the ingredients.

AVOCADO-STUFFED RAINBOW TROUT

4 rainbow trout, cleaned and gutted
sunflower oil for brushing
STUFFING:
1 ripe avocado pear, peeled, stoned and chopped
1 teaspoon lemon juice
25 g (1 oz) pistachio nuts, finely chopped
1 tablespoon clear honey
1 tablespoon soy sauce
salt and pepper
TO GARNISH:
lime slices
coriander leaves

Mix all the stuffing ingredients together, adding salt and pepper to taste. Divide the stuffing between the trout, placing it in the cavity of each fish.

Place the trout in a roasting pan, brush with sunflower oil and cover with foil. Cook in a preheated moderate oven, 180°C (350°F), Gas Mark 4, for 20 minutes or until tender.

Transfer to a warmed serving dish. Garnish with lime and coriander and serve immediately.

Serves 4

STUFFED MUSSELS

4 dozen fresh mussels, scrubbed clean
salt
2 lemon slices
2 teaspoons lemon juice
125 g (4 oz) butter, softened
3 cloves garlic, crushed
1 shallot, finely chopped
2 tablespoons chopped parsley
3 tablespoons fresh wholewheat breadcrumbs
TO GARNISH:
parsley sprigs
lemon wedges

Place the mussels in a pan of boiling salted water, add the lemon slices, cover and cook for about 7 minutes, until the mussels have opened. Remove with a slotted spoon, discarding any that have not opened. Remove the empty top shell from the mussel.

Beat the remaining ingredients together and spread the mixture on top of the mussels.

Place on a baking sheet and cook in a preheated moderately hot oven, 200°C (400°F), Gas Mark 6, for 5 minutes, until golden.

Arrange on a warmed serving dish, garnish with parsley and lemon and serve with crusty French bread.

Serves 4

PRAWN TARTLETS

1 × 215 g (7½ oz) packet frozen wholewheat shortcrust pastry, thawed
3 tablespoons mayonnaise
3 tablespoons soured cream
1 tablespoon tomato ketchup
½ teaspoon Tabasco
1 teaspoon cayenne pepper
2 tablespoons chopped chives
salt and pepper
175 g (6 oz) peeled prawns
7.5 cm (3 inch) piece cucumber, diced
2 tomatoes, skinned and chopped
2 hard-boiled eggs, chopped
dill leaves to garnish

Roll out the pastry on a floured surface to a 5 mm (¼ inch) thickness. Using a 7.5 cm (3 inch) fluted cutter, cut out 24 circles and use to line 2 patty trays. Prick the pastry well and 'bake blind' in a preheated moderate oven, 180°C (350°F), Gas Mark 4, for 10 to 15 minutes, until firm. Cool on a wire rack.

Mix together the mayonnaise, soured cream, tomato ketchup, Tabasco, cayenne, chives, and salt and pepper to taste. Add the remaining ingredients and stir well to mix. Check the seasoning.

Spoon the mixture into the cooked pastry cases. Arrange on a warmed serving dish and garnish with herbs to serve.

Makes 24

SCALLOP AND PRAWN BROCHETTES

150 ml (¼ pint) dry white wine
1 tablespoon raspberry vinegar
1 tablespoon chopped dill weed
½ teaspoon salt
12 large scallops
1½-2 cucumbers, peeled and cut into 1 cm (½ inch) slices
8 Mediterranean prawns
15 g (½ oz) butter, melted
TO GARNISH:
tomato quarters
basil leaves

Place the wine, vinegar, dill weed and salt in a large pan, bring to simmering point and add the scallops and cucumber. Simmer for 1 to 2 minutes, then remove with a slotted spoon; reserve the cooking liquid.

Place a prawn at one end of 4 long kebab skewers, arrange the scallops and cucumber alternately on the skewers, then add another prawn.

Brush with the butter and cook under a preheated high grill, or on a barbecue, for about 3 minutes on each side, basting frequently with the reserved cooking liquid.

Arrange the brochettes on a warmed serving dish. Garnish with tomato and basil and serve with Piquant Tomato Sauce (see page 91).

Serves 4

ICED CUCUMBER AND PRAWN SOUP

25 g (1 oz) butter
1 cucumber, chopped
2 shallots, chopped
300 ml (½ pint) milk
2 cloves garlic, crushed
1 bay leaf
salt and pepper
1 tablespoon chopped mint
1 tablespoon chopped chives
250 g (8 oz) peeled prawns
284 ml (10 fl oz) single cream

TO GARNISH:
mint sprigs
cucumber slices
peeled prawns

Melt the butter in a saucepan, add the cucumber and shallots, cover and cook gently for 5 minutes, until softened but not brown.

Add the milk, garlic, bay leaf, and salt and pepper to taste, and simmer for 10 minutes. Remove the bay leaf. Pour the soup into an electric blender or food processor and work until smooth. Pour into a soup tureen and stir in the herbs, prawns and cream. Chill for 2 hours.

Garnish with mint, cucumber slices and prawns to serve.

Serves 4

VARIATION: This soup could also be served warm: stir in the herbs, prawns and cream as above then heat gently; do not boil.

MONKFISH AND MELON SALAD

1 kg (2 lb) monkfish, cut into strips
8 scallops, cut in half, coral separated
1 onion, chopped
2 lemon or lime slices
bouquet garni
150 ml (1/4 pint) dry cider
150 ml (1/4 pint) water
salt and pepper
SALAD:
1 tablespoon sunflower oil
2 shallots, chopped
6 spring onions, chopped
2.5 cm (1 inch) piece fresh root ginger, chopped
1/2 teaspoon ground ginger
1/2 teaspoon paprika
4 celery sticks, chopped
4 tablespoons soured cream
4 tablespoons mayonnaise
2 tablespoons chopped mint
1 honeydew melon
TO GARNISH:
1/2 teaspoon paprika
lettuce leaves

Place the fish, including the scallop coral, in a pan. Add the remaining ingredients, with salt and pepper to taste, bring to the boil, then simmer for 5 minutes. Drain immediately and leave to cool.

Heat the oil in a pan, add the shallots, spring onions and chopped ginger and sauté for 2 minutes.

Stir in the ground ginger, paprika and celery and cook for 1 minute. Place in a bowl and leave to cool.

Stir in the soured cream, mayonnaise, mint, fish, and salt and pepper to taste.

Halve the melon and discard the seeds. Scoop the flesh into balls, using a melon baller, or cut into cubes, and add to the fish mixture.

Transfer to a serving bowl and chill for 30 minutes, or until required. Sprinkle with paprika and garnish with lettuce to serve.

Serves 4 to 6

NOTE: If preferred, return the salad to the emptied melon shells to serve.

SMOKED EEL MOUSSE

350 g (12 oz) smoked eel
125 g (4 oz) cottage cheese
142 ml (5 fl oz) soured cream
2 teaspoons grated lemon rind
1 tablespoon lemon juice
2 tablespoons chopped parsley
salt and pepper
TO GARNISH:
curly endive leaves
cucumber slices
radish slices

Remove the skin and bones from the eel and flake the fish.

Place in an electric blender or food processor, add the remaining ingredients, with salt and pepper to taste, and work until smooth. Transfer to a bowl and chill until required.

Spoon the mousse onto individual serving plates. Garnish with endive, cucumber and radishes to serve.

Serves 4

POACHED SALMON TROUT

This is an alternative method of cooking a salmon trout if you do not have a fish kettle.

1 salmon trout, weighing about 1 kg (2 lb), cleaned and gutted
1 bay leaf
1 lemon, sliced
1 teaspoon salt
12 black peppercorns
300 ml (½ pint) dry white wine
TO GARNISH:
½ × 25 g (1 oz) packet aspic powder
2 lemons, sliced
2 limes, sliced
small bunch of dill
½ packet of watercress

Line a large roasting pan with foil and brush with oil. Place the salmon trout on the foil, curving the fish slightly. Place the bay leaf and lemon slices on the fish, then sprinkle with the salt and peppercorns. Pour over the wine. Bring the edges of foil together and seal to make a loose parcel.

Cook in a preheated cool oven, 150°C (300°F), Gas Mark 2, for 30 minutes. Leave to cool in the pan.

Unwrap the fish, carefully remove the skin, leaving some around the head and tail, and place on a serving dish.

Make up the aspic to 300 ml (½ pint) according to packet directions. Coat the fish with a thin layer of aspic jelly. Cut most of the lemon and lime slices into quarters and arrange down the centre of the fish with the dill. Brush the lemon and lime slices with a little aspic jelly.

Chill in the refrigerator until set. Garnish with any remaining lemon and lime slices and watercress.

Serves 4

RED MULLET IN VINE LEAVES

6 vine leaves
2 red mullet, weighing about 250 g (8 oz) each, scaled and washed
sunflower oil for brushing
STUFFING:
1 large tomato, chopped
2 anchovy fillets, chopped
2 tablespoons chopped parsley
1 tablespoon chopped basil
1 clove garlic, crushed
salt and pepper
TO GARNISH:
4 anchovies
2 black olives

Mix the stuffing ingredients together, seasoning with salt and pepper, and divide between 2 vine leaves, spreading over one side of each leaf.

Arrange the vine leaves overlapping in two groups of three, with a covered vine leaf forming the centre of each group. Place the mullet on top and wrap the vine leaves around.

Place in a roasting pan, brush with oil and cook in a preheated moderately hot oven, 200°C (400°F), Gas Mark 6, for 15 minutes.

Transfer to a warmed serving dish and top with the anchovies and olives.
Serves 2

SALMON MOUSSE

250 g (8 oz) smoked salmon slices
1 × 439 g (15½ oz) can red salmon
142 ml (5 fl oz) single cream
8 tablespoons crème fraîche
½ cucumber, finely diced
2 tablespoons chopped tarragon
2 eggs, separated
¼ teaspoon cayenne pepper
salt and pepper
15 g (½ oz) gelatine, soaked in 3 tablespoons cold water
watercress or curly endive
lime slices and tarragon leaves to garnish

Line a 1.25 litre (2 ¼ pint) ring mould with the smoked salmon.

Drain and flake the red salmon, then mix with the cream, crème fraîche, cucumber, tarragon, egg yolks, cayenne, and salt and pepper to taste.

Heat the gelatine gently until dissolved, then carefully stir a little at a time into the salmon mixture.

Whisk the egg whites until soft peaks form, then gently fold into the salmon mixture. Pour into the ring mould and chill for several hours, until set.

To serve, invert the ring mould onto a serving plate and fill the centre with watercress or curly endive. Garnish with lime and tarragon.

Serves 6 to 8

GRAPEFRUIT AND PRAWN SALAD

1 tablespoon sunflower oil
1 large onion, finely chopped
250 g (8 oz) peeled prawns
2 tablespoons lemon juice
4 tablespoons dry white wine
salt and pepper
4 tablespoons mayonnaise
1 teaspoon Tabasco
½ teaspoon cayenne pepper
2 ruby red grapefruit, peeled and segmented
1 red pepper, cored, seeded and diced
1 lettuce

Heat the oil in a pan, add the onion and sauté until transparent. Add the prawns, lemon juice, wine, and salt and pepper to taste and simmer for 5 minutes.

Leave to cool slightly, then remove the prawns and onion with a slotted spoon and place in a bowl. Add the mayonnaise, Tabasco and cayenne and stir lightly to mix.

Cut each grapefruit segment in half and add to the prawn mixture with the yellow pepper.

To serve, divide between 4 serving plates, lined with lettuce leaves.
Serves 4

CURRIED PRAWN RING

350 g (12 oz) long grain rice
salt
few saffron threads
1 tablespoon sunflower oil
1 tablespoon curry powder
8 spring onions, chopped
1 red pepper, cored, seeded and chopped
50 g (2 oz) pine nuts
75 g (3 oz) sultanas
250 g (8 oz) peeled prawns

DRESSING:
4 tablespoons olive oil
2 tablespoons white wine vinegar
1 teaspoon dry mustard
1 teaspoon sugar
2 tablespoons chopped coriander

TO GARNISH:
orange wedges
celery leaves

Cook the rice in boiling salted water, with the saffron added, for about 20 minutes, until the rice is tender and the liquid absorbed.

Meanwhile, place the dressing ingredients in a screw-top jar and shake well to blend.

Drain the rice, place in a bowl and stir in the dressing while still warm. Set aside to cool slightly.

Heat the oil in a pan, add the curry powder, spring onions, red pepper, pine nuts and sultanas and cook, stirring, for 1½ minutes. Add to the rice and leave until completely cold.

Stir in the prawns, then spoon the mixture into a lightly oiled 1.5 litre (2½ pint) ring mould, pressing down well. Chill until required.

To serve, invert the ring onto a serving plate and garnish with orange wedges and celery leaves.

Serves 4 to 6

JOHN DORY FILLETS

25 g (1 oz) plain flour
salt and pepper
6 John Dory fillets
175 g (6 oz) butter
350 g (12 oz) mushrooms, sliced
1 clove garlic, crushed
8 tablespoons double cream
1 teaspoon lemon juice

TO GARNISH:
parsley sprigs
lemon wedges

Season the flour with salt and pepper and use to coat the fish.

Heat 125 g (4 oz) of the butter in a small pan until bubbling. Line a sieve with muslin and pour the butter through this into a frying pan. Add the fish and fry gently for 3 minutes on each side. Keep warm.

Melt the remaining butter in another pan, add the mushrooms and garlic, cover and simmer for 8 minutes. Stir in the cream, lemon juice, and salt and pepper to taste and heat gently.

Arrange the fish on a warmed serving dish and pour over the sauce. Garnish with parsley and lemon wedges to serve.

Serves 6

SEA BASS BAKED IN SPINACH

1 sea bass, weighing about 750 g (1½ lb), cleaned and gutted
250 g (8 oz) spinach
15 g (½ oz) butter, melted
2 shallots, chopped
150 ml (¼ pint) dry white wine

STUFFING:
50 g (2 oz) fresh breadcrumbs
15 g (½ oz) butter, melted
2 tablespoons chopped chervil
1 tablespoon each chopped tarragon and basil
1 tablespoon lemon juice
salt and pepper

TO GARNISH:
3 orange slices, quartered

Mix the stuffing ingredients together, seasoning with salt and pepper to taste, and use to stuff the fish cavity.

Put the spinach in a colander in a bowl and pour over boiling water. Drain thoroughly.

Wrap the stuffed bass in the blanched spinach, leaving the head and tail exposed.

Pour the melted butter over the base of a gratin dish, sprinkle in the shallots and place the fish on top. Pour over the wine.

Cover with foil and cook in a preheated moderately hot oven, 200°C (400°F), Gas Mark 6, for 30 minutes.

Transfer to a warmed serving dish, garnish with quartered orange slices and serve with a sauce (see pages 84-91) if preferred.

Serves 2

FISH CASSEROLE

1 dozen mussels, cleaned
salt and pepper
1 monkfish, cleaned and filleted
2 squid, cleaned and ink sac removed
2 tablespoons oil
2 onions, chopped
2 carrots, thinly sliced
6 celery sticks, sliced
2 cloves garlic, crushed
1 × 397 g (14 oz) can tomatoes
2 teaspoons sugar
2 tablespoons lemon juice
2 tablespoons lime juice
2 tablespoons chopped coriander
bouquet garni
150 ml (1/4 pint) dry cider
few drops of Tabasco
4 scallops, cleaned and cut in half horizontally
3 small red mullet, scaled and cleaned
chopped coriander to garnish

Place the mussels in a pan of boiling salted water and cook for about 7 minutes, until they open; discard any that do not open.

Cut the monkfish into 2.5 cm (1 inch) chunks. Cut the squid into thin slices; leave the tentacles in small pieces.

Heat the oil in a large pan, add the onions, carrots, celery and garlic and sauté for 4 minutes. Add the remaining ingredients, except the fish, with salt and pepper to taste, and bring to the boil. Add all the fish except the mussels, cover and simmer for 15 to 20 minutes, until the fish is cooked. Discard the bouquet garni.

Stir in the mussels and transfer to a warmed serving dish. Sprinkle with coriander and serve immediately.

Serves 6

SOLE VÉRONIQUE

8 Dover sole fillets
2 shallots, finely sliced
2 button mushrooms, finely sliced
1 bay leaf
1 parsley sprig
4 lemon slices
150 ml (¼ pint) dry white wine
4 tablespoons water
150 ml (¼ pint) milk (approximately)
25 g (1 oz) butter
25 g (1 oz) plain flour
142 ml (5 fl oz) double cream
1 teaspoon lemon juice
salt and pepper
175 g (6 oz) green grapes, peeled, cut in half and pips removed

Place the fish in a buttered ovenproof dish and sprinkle with the shallots and mushrooms. Add the bay leaf, parsley and lemon slices, and pour in the wine and water.

Cover with foil and cook in a preheated moderate oven, 180°C (350°F), Gas Mark 4, for 15 to 20 minutes, until tender.

Transfer the fish to a heatproof serving dish; keep warm.

Strain the cooking liquid into a small pan, bring to the boil and boil rapidly until reduced by half. Pour into a measuring jug and make up to 300 ml (½ pint) with the milk.

Melt the butter in a pan, stir in the flour and cook for 1 minute. Gradually stir in the reserved cooking liquid and milk mixture, bring to the boil, then simmer for 2 to 3 minutes. Stir in the cream, lemon juice, and salt and pepper to taste and bring to just below boiling point.

Remove from the heat and stir in two thirds of the grapes. Pour over the fish. Place under a preheated moderate grill for 1 minute to brown.

Garnish with the remaining grapes.

Serves 4

BRILL WITH PEAR

1 × 213 g (7½ oz) can pear halves in natural juice
4 brill or small turbot fillets
1 egg yolk
2 tablespoons chopped tarragon
1 tablespoon chopped parsley
1 teaspoon grated lemon rind
salt and pepper
142 ml (5 fl oz) single cream

Drain the pears and cut each piece in half. Wrap one fish fillet around each pear quarter. Place in a buttered ovenproof dish, just large enough to hold the fillets.

Beat the egg yolk, herbs, lemon rind, and salt and pepper to taste into the cream. Pour over the fish.

Cover with foil and cook in a preheated moderate oven, 180°C (350°F), Gas Mark 4, for 25 minutes or until tender. Serve hot.

Serves 4

BARBECUED SARDINES

These are excellent to serve at barbecue parties. They can, of course, also be cooked under a traditional grill.

16 fresh sardines, cleaned
MARINADE:
8 tablespoons lemon juice
2 tablespoons lime juice
3 cloves garlic, crushed
1 teaspoon paprika
1 teaspoon ground ginger
1 teaspoon ground cumin
1 teaspoon tomato purée
TO GARNISH:
lime slices
basil sprigs

Place the sardines in a flat dish. Mix the marinade ingredients together and pour over the fish. Leave to marinate in the refrigerator for 1 hour. Remove with a slotted spoon, reserving the marinade.

Line a grill pan with greased foil and place the sardines in the pan.

Cook under a preheated grill for 5 minutes on each side, basting with the marinade. Garnish with lime and basil. Accompany with Spicy Gooseberry Sauce (see page 88).
Serves 8

GOUJONS OF SOLE

2 Dover sole, skinned and filleted
50 g (2 oz) hazelnuts, finely chopped
125 g (4 oz) fresh wholewheat breadcrumbs
25 g (1 oz) plain flour
salt and pepper
1-2 eggs, beaten
oil for deep-frying
TO GARNISH:
parsley sprigs
orange segments

Cut the sole diagonally into strips about 2.5 cm (1 inch) wide.

Mix together the hazelnuts and breadcrumbs in a bowl.

Season the flour with salt and pepper and use to coat the fish. Dip into the beaten egg, then roll in the breadcrumb mixture to coat completely. Chill for about 30 minutes.

Deep-fry in hot oil, a few at a time, for 2 minutes, until crisp and golden. Drain on kitchen paper and place in a warmed serving dish.

Garnish with parsley and orange and serve immediately, accompanied by Tartare Sauce (see page 89) and a crisp green salad.

Serves 2 to 4

SOLE FILLETS WITH COURGETTES

50 g (2 oz) unsalted butter
350 g (12 oz) small courgettes, thinly sliced
salt and pepper
1 large tomato, skinned, seeded and chopped
4 Dover sole fillets
2 tablespoons lemon juice
1 tablespoon chopped basil
1 tablespoon fresh breadcrumbs
basil leaves to garnish

Melt half the butter in a pan, add the courgettes, and salt and pepper to taste and sauté for 3 minutes.

Add the tomato and continue cooking for 3 minutes, stirring occasionally.

Place the sole fillets in a gratin dish, dot with the remaining butter, and season with salt and pepper to taste. Pour over the lemon juice and sprinkle with the basil.

Pour the tomato and courgette mixture evenly over the fish and sprinkle with the breadcrumbs. Cook in a preheated moderately hot oven, 200°C (400°F), Gas Mark 6, for 10 to 15 minutes, until the fish is tender and the breadcrumbs crisp and golden.

Garnish with basil to serve.

Serves 2 or 4

OYSTERS

Oysters are very good on their own – *au naturel*. To ensure they are at their freshest, open them when you are about to serve the dish.

To open oysters, use a special oyster knife, if possible, or a round short-bladed knife; don't use a good sharp knife – you'll ruin it.

To protect your palm from the rough-edged shells, scrub them first and place a cloth in your palm. Holding the oyster over a bowl to catch the juice, insert the knife into the hinge and twist around between the shells to prise open. When breaking the shell open, try to keep the oyster in one piece by cutting the two muscles which lie above and below it.

To serve oysters *au naturel*, serve them on the flat shell on a bed of crushed ice, garnished with seaweed if possible for authenticity. Season lightly with salt and pepper and serve with lemon wedges and brown bread and butter.

OYSTERS À LA CRÈME

12 oysters
15 g (½ oz) butter
1 shallot, finely chopped
1 teaspoon chopped chervil
142 ml (5 fl oz) double cream
salt and pepper
25 g (1 oz) Gruyère cheese, grated
1 tablespoon dried breadcrumbs
chervil sprigs and lemon wedges to garnish

Open the oysters as described opposite. Return the oysters to the deeper rounded shell and arrange on a baking sheet, keeping them level with foil.

Melt the butter in a small pan, add the shallot and sauté until soft. Stir in the chervil, cream, and salt and pepper to taste and gently bring to the boil. Remove from the heat and stir in the cheese.

Cover each oyster with the sauce and sprinkle with the breadcrumbs.

Place under a preheated moderate grill for 2 minutes, until golden brown. Garnish with chervil and lemon and serve immediately.

Serves 2 to 4

OYSTERS WITH SMOKED SALMON

12 oysters
75 g (3 oz) smoked salmon, finely chopped
½ × 397 g (14 oz) can artichoke hearts, drained and finely chopped
25 g (1 oz) Gruyère cheese, grated
2 tablespoons dried breadcrumbs
pepper
HERB BUTTER:
75 g (3 oz) butter, softened
1 tablespoon chopped chervil
1 tablespoon chopped tarragon
2 teaspoons lemon juice
TO GARNISH:
lime wedges
tarragon leaves

First make the herb butter by beating all the ingredients together in a small bowl.

Open the oysters as described opposite. Return the oysters to the deeper rounded shell.

Place a little chopped salmon and artichoke on each oyster and dot with the herb butter. Sprinkle with the cheese, breadcrumbs, and pepper to taste.

Place on a baking sheet, balancing the oyster shells with foil if necessary, and cook in a preheated moderately hot oven, 200°C (400°F), Gas Mark 6, for 15 minutes. Alternatively, place under a preheated moderate grill for 10 to 15 minutes, until golden.

Transfer to a warmed serving dish, garnish with lime wedges and tarragon leaves and serve with brown bread and butter.

Serves 2 to 4

DRESSED CRAB

These days, dressed crab is quite readily available in the shops. However if you should have to cook and dress a live crab, here's how to go about it.

To Cook a Crab
Weigh the crab, if possible!

Have ready a large saucepan full of boiling salted water: use 175 g (6 oz) salt to 2-2.5 litres (3½-4 pints) water. Add a bay leaf, 5 peppercorns, 1 sliced onion, and 2 sliced celery sticks.

Put the crab in the water, cover the pan and bring to simmering point. Cook, allowing 15 minutes for the first 500 g (1 lb) and 8 minutes for each additional 500 g (1 lb). Remove from the pan and leave until cool.

To Dress a Crab
1. Place the crab on its back. Using a twisting action, remove the legs and claws from the body and set aside.
2. To separate the body, have the tail flap towards you. Hold the shell firmly with your fingers and, using your thumbs, push the body upwards until it becomes loosened, then separate from the shell.
3. Remove and discard the intestines or stomach bag and the grey feathery gills known as 'dead man's fingers'.
4. Spoon out the brown meat from the shell and place in a dish.
5. Cut the body in half. Using a thin skewer, dig out the white meat from the crevices. This may take time and patience, but is well worth it. Place in a separate dish.
6. Carefully crack open the reserved claws and legs using the back of a wooden spoon or a rolling pin and remove all the white meat; don't hit too hard or you will break up the meat. Add to the other white meat.
7. Trim the crab shell by tapping gently with a spoon around the natural marked line on the shell. Clean the shell ready for serving.

To Serve a Crab
Finely chop the white meat and season to taste with salt and pepper, cayenne pepper and 1 teaspoon dry white wine or cider vinegar.

Mix the brown meat with salt and pepper to taste, 1 teaspoon gin (optional), and 1 tablespoon finely chopped parsley (optional).

Place the brown meat in the centre of the shell and the white meat on either side. Garnish with chopped hard-boiled egg yolk and white, and 2 tablespoons finely chopped parsley, as shown.

Serve with an avocado and lettuce salad and mayonnaise.

Serves 2 to 4, depending on size of crab.

DEVILLED CRAB

2 crabs
142 ml (5 fl oz) double cream or crème fraîche
1 teaspoon Dijon mustard
2 teaspoons anchovy essence
1 teaspoon Worcestershire sauce
½ teaspoon cayenne pepper
1 teaspoon lemon juice
2 tablespoons chopped parsley
1 teaspoon chopped marjoram
125 g (4 oz) tomatoes, skinned and chopped
2 tablespoons dry sherry
salt and pepper
2 tablespoons fresh breadcrumbs, toasted
2 tablespoons finely grated Cheshire cheese
TO GARNISH:
watercress
cucumber slices

Cook and dress the crabs as described on page 76 and place all the meat in a large bowl. Stir in the cream or crème fraîche, mustard, anchovy essence, Worcestershire sauce, cayenne, lemon juice, parsley, marjoram, tomatoes, sherry, and salt and pepper to taste.

Brush the cleaned crab shells, inside and out, with oil. Divide the mixture between the shells; put any leftover mixture in a ramekin dish. Sprinkle with the breadcrumbs and cheese and cook in a preheated moderately hot oven, 200°C (400°F), Gas Mark 6, for 15 to 20 minutes, until golden brown.

To serve, place on a bed of lettuce and garnish with watercress and cucumber slices.

Serves 4

CRAB AND HERB MOUSSE

250 g (8 oz) crabmeat, fresh, frozen or canned
2 tablespoons finely grated Cheddar cheese
142 ml (5 fl oz) double cream
2 tablespoons chopped tarragon
1 tablespoon chopped chervil
1 tablespoon chopped basil
1 tablespoon lemon juice
1 tablespoon tomato ketchup
salt and pepper
15 g (½ oz) gelatine, soaked in 3 tablespoons cold water
2 egg whites
TO GARNISH:
cucumber slices
whole prawn in shell

Flake the crabmeat finely and place in a bowl. Stir in the cheese, cream, herbs, lemon juice, tomato ketchup, and salt and pepper to taste.

Heat the gelatine gently until dissolved, then carefully fold into the crab mixture.

Whisk the egg whites until soft peaks form, then fold into the crab mixture using a metal spoon.

Spoon the mixture into an 18-20 cm (7-8 inch) round cake tin or mould and chill for several hours, until set.

To serve, invert the mould onto a serving plate and garnish with cucumber slices and a whole prawn.

Serves 6

LOBSTERS

Lobsters are usually sold ready-cooked, but ideally they should be purchased alive. The shells are then greyish-blue – they turn their characteristic bright red colour in cooking. Smaller lobsters – about 750 g-1 kg (1½-2 lb) – have the best flavour. When selecting for buying, choose a lobster which feels heavy for its size.

To Cook a Lobster
Have ready a large saucepan full of boiling salted water: use 175 g (6 oz) salt to about 2 litres (3½ pints) water. Put the lobster in the water, cover the pan and bring to simmering point. Alternatively, if serving the lobster plain, cook in a court-bouillon (see page 11). Cook, allowing 12-15 minutes for the first 500 g (1 lb) and 10 minutes for each additional 500 g (1 lb).

To Prepare a Lobster
1. Remove the red, cooked lobster from the pan. Place the lobster on its back and remove the legs and claws with a twisting action. Using the back of a wooden spoon, crack them open and carefully remove the meat. Remove the flesh, intact if possible, from the claws.
2. Turn the lobster over. Using a sharp knife, draw it through the head from the shoulder up towards the eye. Now cut along the centre of the body to the tail, splitting the lobster into two halves.
3. Remove and discard the white gills, the dark intestinal vein which goes along into the tail, and the small stomach sac, which lies in the head. Don't discard the green creamy liver in the head: it is a delicacy. Use it to make lobster sauce.

If you buy a female lobster, she may have an excellent red coral or roe, which can also be used in sauces.
4. Extract the white meat from the lobster and use as desired. To serve *au naturel*, cut the white meat into neat slices and place all the lobster meat in the cleaned shells or arrange attractively on a serving plate. Serve cold with mayonnaise or vinaigrette and a salad. Alternatively, place under a preheated moderate grill for a few minutes and serve warm with melted butter.

LOBSTER WITH TOMATO SAUCE

2 lobsters, about 500-750 g (1-1½ lb) each
25 g (1 oz) butter
1 tablespoon dry sherry
TOMATO SAUCE:
1 tablespoon sunflower oil
1 onion, finely chopped
1 carrot, finely chopped
2 cloves garlic, crushed
1 × 793 g (1 lb 12 oz) can tomatoes or 1 kg (2 lb) fresh tomatoes, skinned
1 teaspoon sugar
150 ml (¼ pint) dry red wine
salt and pepper
½ teaspoon chilli powder
½ teaspoon cayenne pepper
TO GARNISH:
lime wedges
basil sprigs

First make the tomato sauce. Heat the oil in a pan, add the onion and carrot and fry until golden. Add the garlic, tomatoes with their juice, sugar, wine, and salt and pepper to taste. Bring to the boil, stirring with a wooden spoon to break up the tomatoes, then simmer for 20 to 30 minutes, until thickened.

Rub through a sieve, or work in an electric blender or food processor, and return to the pan. Stir in the chilli powder and cayenne pepper.

Prepare the lobster as described opposite and slice the meat into pieces. Clean the shells and set aside.

Add the lobster meat to the warm tomato sauce and heat through. Stir in the butter and sherry. Return to the shells or place on a serving plate.

Garnish with lime wedges and basil to serve.

Serves 4 to 6

LOBSTER THERMIDOR

450 ml (¾ pint) milk
1 onion, cut into quarters
1 bay leaf
bouquet garni
150 ml (¼ pint) dry white wine
3 cooked lobsters, about 500-750 g (1-1½ lb) each
125 g (4 oz) unsalted butter
50 g (2 oz) plain flour
2 teaspoons Dijon mustard
2 large egg yolks
142 ml (5 fl oz) single cream
2 teaspoons lemon juice
2 tablespoons finely chopped parsley
salt and pepper

TOPPING:

50 g (2 oz) fresh breadcrumbs
75 g (3 oz) Parmesan cheese, grated

TO GARNISH:

lemon or lime wedges
parsley sprigs

Pour the milk into a saucepan and add the onion, bay leaf and bouquet garni. Bring to the boil, then remove from the heat and leave to infuse for 30 minutes.

Place the wine in a small pan and boil for 3 minutes to reduce.

Prepare the lobsters as described on page 80. Cut the meat into 1 cm (½ inch) pieces and set aside. Sieve any coral and set aside. Clean the shells and set aside.

Melt half the butter in a frying pan, add the lobster meat and cook gently, stirring, for 2 minutes. Remove from the heat.

Melt the remaining butter in another pan, stir in the flour and cook for 1 minute. Remove from the heat.

Strain the infused milk, then gradually beat into the roux. Add the reduced wine, bring gently to the boil, then simmer for 4 minutes. Leave to cool then stir in the mustard, egg yolks, coral, if present, cream, lemon juice, parsley, and salt and pepper to taste. Spoon a little of this sauce into the bottom of each lobster shell.

Add the lobster meat to the remaining sauce and stir gently. Spoon into the shells and sprinkle with the breadcrumbs and cheese.

Place on a baking sheet and cook in a preheated moderately hot oven, 200°C (400°F), Gas Mark 6, for 7 to 10 minutes, until golden brown. Garnish with lemon or lime wedges and parsley. Serve immediately.

Serves 6

SAUCES AND ACCOMPANIMENTS

Many fish dishes are enhanced by accompanying sauces and savoury butters. Here you will find plenty of ideas to choose from. These accompaniments are quick and easy to prepare – and well worth the effort. The butters and cold sauces can be prepared well ahead and stored in the refrigerator until required.

GOOSEBERRY SAUCE

500 g (1 lb) gooseberries
2 tablespoons water
25 g (1 oz) butter
1 tablespoon demerara sugar
1 egg
salt and white pepper

Place the gooseberries and water in a pan, bring to the boil, then simmer for 20 minutes. Stir in the butter and sugar.

Whisk the egg until pale and fluffy, using an electric blender or beater. Carefully pour the hot gooseberries onto the egg, while the motor is running, to form an emulsion. Season with salt and pepper. Serve hot or cold with mackerel or herring.

Makes 350 ml (12 fl oz)

CHAMPAGNE SAUCE

This is a delicious sauce, worth making for a special occasion. It is traditionally served with shellfish, such as lobster, scallops and crayfish.

25 g (1 oz) unsalted butter
3 shallots, finely chopped
300 ml (½ pint) champagne
284 ml (10 fl oz) single cream
salt and pepper
2 tablespoons finely chopped chervil (optional)
2 tablespoons finely chopped tarragon (optional)
50 g (2 oz) mushrooms, finely sliced (optional)

Melt the butter in a pan, stir in the shallots and fry for 5 minutes, until softened.

Pour in the champagne, bring to the boil, and boil gently for about 15 minutes, until reduced by half. Remove from the heat and cool slightly. Stir in the cream, add salt and pepper to taste, return to the heat and heat gently until thick enough to coat the back of a spoon. Stir in the herbs and mushrooms, if using.

Serve hot, with shellfish or poached salmon.

Makes 350 ml (12 fl oz)

WHITE SAUCE

25 g (1 oz) butter
25 g (1 oz) plain flour
300 ml (½ pint) milk
salt and pepper

Melt the butter in a pan, stir in the flour and cook, stirring, for 1 minute. Remove from the heat and gradually beat in the milk, and salt and pepper to taste. Return to the heat, bring to the boil and cook for 2 minutes, stirring constantly.

Serve hot with plaice, haddock, cod.

Makes 300 ml (½ pint)

VARIATIONS:

Parsley Sauce: Stir 50 g (2 oz) chopped parsley into the finished sauce.

Cheese Sauce: Stir 75 g (3 oz) grated Cheddar cheese and 1 teaspoon dry mustard into the finished sauce.

Mushroom Sauce: Sauté 50 g (2 oz) sliced mushrooms in 15 g (½ oz) butter with 1 teaspoon lemon juice for 5 minutes. Stir into the finished sauce.

Onion Sauce: Sauté 1 finely chopped onion in the butter for 7 minutes, before stirring in the flour.

Caper Sauce: Stir 1 tablespoon finely chopped capers and 1 teaspoon lemon juice into the finished sauce.

Prawn Sauce: Stir 75 g (3 oz) peeled prawns and ½ teaspoon cayenne pepper into the finished sauce.

BÉCHAMEL SAUCE

300 ml (½ pint) milk
1 small onion, quartered
1 bay leaf
2 thyme sprigs
1 parsley sprig
pinch of grated nutmeg
salt and pepper
25 g (1 oz) butter
25 g (1 oz) plain flour

Pour the milk into a saucepan and add the onion, herbs, nutmeg, and salt and pepper to taste. Bring slowly to the boil, remove from the heat at once, cover and leave to infuse for 30 minutes to 1 hour, then strain.

Melt the butter in a pan, stir in the flour and cook, stirring, for 1 minute. Remove from the heat and gradually stir in the strained milk. Return to the heat, bring to the boil and cook for 2 minutes, stirring constantly. Check the seasoning.

Makes 300 ml (½ pint)

MUSTARD SAUCE

1 large egg yolk
2 tablespoons Dijon mustard
½ teaspoon sugar
1 tablespoon wine vinegar
6 tablespoons oil
salt and pepper
1 tablespoon chopped dill

Beat the egg yolk with the mustard and sugar until smooth. Stir in the vinegar. Gradually beat in the oil and add salt and pepper to taste. Stir in the dill. Serve cold.

Makes 120 ml (4 fl oz)

FRESH HERB SAUCE

2 packets of watercress
1 bunch of parsley
2 tarragon sprigs
4 chervil sprigs
2 tablespoons lemon juice
4 tablespoons oil
350 g (12 oz) fromage blanc

Finely chop the watercress and herbs and place in a bowl. Gradually stir in the lemon juice and oil, then the fromage blanc. Season with salt and pepper to taste.

Serve warm, heated very gently, or cold, with scallops and trout fillets.

Makes 450 ml (¾ pint)

SPICY GOOSEBERRY SAUCE

500 g (1 lb) gooseberries
1 clove garlic, crushed
1 teaspoon salt
2 teaspoons dry mustard
150 ml (¼ pint) white wine vinegar
175 g (6 oz) demerara sugar
50 g (2 oz) sultanas
150 ml (¼ pint) water

Place all the ingredients in a saucepan, bring to the boil, stirring, then simmer for 40 minutes, stirring occasionally. Cool slightly, then place in an electric blender or food processor and work until smooth; rub through a sieve to remove the pips.

Serve hot or cold. Delicious with baked herring and mackerel.

Makes 350 ml (12 fl oz)

TARTARE SAUCE

4 teaspoons capers
3 cocktail gherkins
a few chives
150 ml (¼ pint) mayonnaise
2 tablespoons yogurt

Chop the capers, gherkins and chives. Mix all the ingredients together. Serve cold.

Makes 200 ml (⅓ pint)

HORSERADISH AND DILL SAUCE

2 tablespoons grated horseradish
2 tablespoons lemon juice
1 small dessert apple, peeled, cored and grated
142 ml (5 fl oz) soured cream
1 tablespoon chopped dill
salt and pepper

Stir the horseradish, lemon juice and apple into the soured cream.

Add the dill, and salt and pepper to taste.

Serve hot or cold. To serve hot, heat through very gently; do not allow to boil.

Makes 150 ml (¼ pint)

TOMATO SAUCE

1 tablespoon oil
50 g (2 oz) mushrooms, finely chopped
1 onion, finely chopped
1 clove garlic, crushed
1 × 397 g (14 oz) can chopped tomatoes
6 tablespoons red wine
1 teaspoon tomato purée
1 bay leaf
salt and pepper

Heat the oil in a pan, add the mushrooms and onion and sauté for 3 minutes, until softened.

Add the remaining ingredients, with salt and pepper to taste, bring to the boil, then simmer for 20 to 30 minutes, stirring occasionally, until the desired consistency. Remove the bay leaf.

Makes about 300 ml (½ pint)

HOLLANDAISE SAUCE

3 tablespoons white wine vinegar
1 tablespoon water
6 peppercorns
1 bay leaf
3 egg yolks
175 g (6 oz) unsalted butter, cut into cubes
salt and white pepper
1 teaspoon lemon juice (optional)

Place the vinegar, water, peppercorns and bay leaf in a pan, bring to the boil and boil until reduced to approximately 1 tablespoon liquid.

Place the egg yolks and 15 g (½ oz) of the butter in a heatproof bowl and cream until soft. Strain in the vinegar.

Place the bowl over a pan two-thirds filled with boiling water. Beat in the cubes of butter one at a time, mixing thoroughly until the sauce is creamy and shiny. If it refuses to thicken, turn the heat up a little; if it shows signs of thickening too soon or curdling, remove it from the pan and place in a bowl of cold water, stirring all the time. Stir in salt and pepper and lemon juice, if using.

Serve warm. Ideal with poached salmon, trout and baked sea bass.

Makes 300 ml (½ pint)

PIQUANT TOMATO SAUCE

1 kg (2 lb) tomatoes, roughly chopped
4 shallots, chopped
½ carrot, grated
4 tablespoons orange juice
1 teaspoon grated orange rind
1 teaspoon salt
1½ tablespoons sugar
1 teaspoon paprika

Place all the ingredients in a saucepan, bring to the boil, then simmer for 15 minutes. Rub through a fine sieve to form a smooth sauce.

Serve hot or cold. Excellent served with scallops or Scallop and Prawn Brochettes (see page 58).

Makes 600 ml (1 pint)

EASY HOLLANDAISE SAUCE

If you have problems with traditional Hollandaise Sauce, this is an easier version, which tastes just as good.

15 g (½ oz) butter
15 g (½ oz) plain flour
150 ml (¼ pint) hot water (not boiling)
2 egg yolks
125 g (4 oz) butter, cut into cubes
1 tablespoon lemon juice
salt and white pepper

Melt the butter in a pan, stir in the flour and cook, stirring, for 1 minute. Remove from the heat and gradually beat in the water. Return to the heat and gradually whisk in the egg yolks. Heat gently, whisking constantly, until the mixture begins to thicken. Remove from the heat and gently beat in the butter, one cube at a time. Stir in the lemon juice, and salt and pepper to taste.

Makes 300 ml (½ pint)

SAVOURY BUTTERS

These are excellent accompaniments to serve either melted or chilled, with fish.

Anchovy Butter

6 anchovy fillets
125 g (4 oz) unsalted butter, softened
1 teaspoon anchovy essence

Rinse the anchovies in cold water; dry thoroughly. Chop finely, then rub through a sieve. Beat into the butter with the anchovy essence.

Serve with grilled fish and herrings.

Tarragon Butter

50 g (2 oz) tarragon
125 g (4 oz) unsalted butter, softened

Finely chop the tarragon and beat into the butter. Serve on top of a hot turbot steak.

Pear Butter

1 × 213 g (7½ oz) can pear halves in natural juice, drained
125 g (4 oz) unsalted butter, softened
pepper

Place the pears in an electric blender or food processor and work until smooth. Beat in the butter and season with pepper to taste.

Serve on rye bread with smoked salmon.

Maître d'Hôtel Butter

1 tablespoon finely chopped parsley
1 teaspoon grated lemon rind
1 tablespoon lemon juice
125 g (4 oz) unsalted butter, softened
salt and pepper

Beat all the ingredients together, seasoning with salt and pepper to taste.

Serve with grilled fish, eg skate wings.

INDEX

ACKNOWLEDGMENTS
Photography by Clive Streeter
Food prepared by Clare Gordon-Smith
Photographic stylist: Gina Carminati